ELLA FITZGERALD

ELLA FITZGERALD

— ◆ —

Bud Kliment

DISCARD

Senior Consulting Editor
Nathan Irvin Huggins
Director
W.E.B. Du Bois Institute for Afro-American Research
Harvard University

CHELSEA HOUSE PUBLISHERS
New York   Philadelphia

Chelsea House Publishers

Editor-in-Chief   Nancy Toff
Executive Editor   Remmel T. Nunn
Managing Editor   Karyn Gullen Browne
Copy Chief   Juliann Barbato
Picture Editor   Adrian G. Allen
Art Director   Giannella Garrett
Manufacturing Manager   Gerald Levine

Black Americans of Achievement

Senior Editor   Richard Rennert

Staff for ELLA FITZGERALD

Associate Editor   Perry King
Assistant Editor   Gillian Bucky
Editorial Assistant   Susan DeRosa
Deputy Copy Chief   Ellen Scordato
Associate Picture Editor   Juliette Dickstein
Picture Researcher   Lisa Kirchner
Senior Designer   Laurie Jewell
Designer   Victoria Tomaselli
Production Coordinator   Joseph Romano
Cover Illustration   Alan J. Nahigian

9

Library of Congress Cataloging in Publication Data

Kliment, Bud.
  Ella Fitzgerald.

  (Black Americans of Achievement)
  Bibliography: p.
  Includes index.
  1. Fitzgerald, Ella. 2. Singers—United States—
Biography. I. Title. II. Series.
ML420.F52K6   1988   784.5 [B]   88-9530
ISBN 1-55546-586-2
    0-7910-0220-9 (pbk.)

CONTENTS

BLACK AMERICANS OF ACHIEVEMENT

RALPH ABERNATHY
civil rights leader

MUHAMMAD ALI
heavyweight champion

RICHARD ALLEN
religious leader and social activist

LOUIS ARMSTRONG
musician

ARTHUR ASHE
tennis great

JOSEPHINE BAKER
entertainer

JAMES BALDWIN
author

BENJAMIN BANNEKER
scientist and mathematician

AMIRI BARAKA
poet and playwright

COUNT BASIE
bandleader and composer

ROMARE BEARDEN
artist

JAMES BECKWOURTH
frontiersman

MARY MCLEOD
BETHUNE
educator

BLANCHE BRUCE
politician

RALPH BUNCHE
diplomat

GEORGE WASHINGTON
CARVER
botanist

CHARLES CHESNUTT
author

BILL COSBY
entertainer

PAUL CUFFE
merchant and abolitionist

FATHER DIVINE
religious leader

FREDERICK DOUGLASS
abolitionist editor

CHARLES DREW
physician

W.E.B. DU BOIS
scholar and activist

PAUL LAURENCE DUNBAR
poet

KATHERINE DUNHAM
dancer and choreographer

MARIAN WRIGHT EDELMAN
civil rights leader and lawyer

DUKE ELLINGTON
bandleader and composer

RALPH ELLISON
author

JULIUS ERVING
basketball great

JAMES FARMER
civil rights leader

ELLA FITZGERALD
singer

MARCUS GARVEY
black-nationalist leader

DIZZY GILLESPIE
musician

PRINCE HALL
social reformer

W. C. HANDY
father of the blues

WILLIAM HASTIE
educator and politician

MATTHEW HENSON
explorer

CHESTER HIMES
author

BILLIE HOLIDAY
singer

JOHN HOPE
educator

LENA HORNE
entertainer

LANGSTON HUGHES
poet

ZORA NEALE HURSTON
author

JESSE JACKSON
civil rights leader and politician

JACK JOHNSON
heavyweight champion

JAMES WELDON JOHNSON
author

SCOTT JOPLIN
composer

BARBARA JORDAN
politician

MARTIN LUTHER KING, JR.
civil rights leader

ALAIN LOCKE
scholar and educator

JOE LOUIS
heavyweight champion

RONALD MCNAIR
astronaut

MALCOLM X
militant black leader

THURGOOD MARSHALL
Supreme Court justice

ELIJAH MUHAMMAD
religious leader

JESSE OWENS
champion athlete

CHARLIE PARKER
musician

GORDON PARKS
photographer

SIDNEY POITIER
actor

ADAM CLAYTON POWELL, JR.
political leader

LEONTYNE PRICE
opera singer

A. PHILIP RANDOLPH
labor leader

PAUL ROBESON
singer and actor

JACKIE ROBINSON
baseball great

BILL RUSSELL
basketball great

JOHN RUSSWURM
publisher

SOJOURNER TRUTH
antislavery activist

HARRIET TUBMAN
antislavery activist

NAT TURNER
slave revolt leader

DENMARK VESEY
slave revolt leader

MADAM C. J. WALKER
entrepreneur

BOOKER T. WASHINGTON
educator

HAROLD WASHINGTON
politician

WALTER WHITE
civil rights leader and author

RICHARD WRIGHT
author

ON ACHIEVEMENT

Coretta Scott King

BEFORE YOU BEGIN this book, I hope you will ask yourself what the word excellence means to you. I think that it's a question we should all ask, and keep asking as we grow older and change. Because the truest answer to it should never change. When you think of excellence, perhaps you think of success at work; or of becoming wealthy; or meeting the right person, getting married, and having a good family life.

Those important goals are worth striving for, but there is a better way to look at excellence. As Martin Luther King, Jr., said in one of his last sermons, "I want you to be first in love. I want you to be first in moral excellence. I want you to be first in generosity. If you want to be important, wonderful. If you want to be great, wonderful. But recognize that he who is greatest among you shall be your servant."

My husband, Martin Luther King, Jr., knew that the true meaning of achievement is service. When I met him, in 1952, he was already ordained as a Baptist preacher and was working towards a doctoral degree at Boston University. I was studying at the New England Conservatory and dreamed of accomplishments in music. We married a year later, and after I graduated the following year we moved to Montgomery, Alabama. We didn't know it then, but our notions of achievement were about to undergo a dramatic change.

You may have read or heard about what happened next. What began with the boycott of a local bus line grew into a national movement, and by the time he was assassinated in 1968 my husband had fashioned a black movement powerful enough to shatter forever the practice of racial segregation. What you may not have read about is where he got his method for resisting injustice without compromising his religious beliefs.

He got the strategy of nonviolence from a man of a different race, who lived in a distant country, and even practiced a different religion. The man was Mahatma Gandhi, the great leader of India, who devoted his life to serving humanity in the spirit of love and nonviolence. It was in these principles that Martin discovered his method for social reform. More than anything else, those two principles were the key to his achievements.

This book is about black Americans who served society through the excellence of their achievements. It forms a part of the rich history of black men and women in America—a history of stunning accomplishments in every field of human endeavor, from literature and art to science, industry, education, diplomacy, athletics, jurisprudence, even polar exploration.

Not all of the people in this history had the same ideals, but I think you will find something that all of them have in common. Like Martin Luther King, Jr., they all decided to become "drum majors" and serve humanity. In that principle—whether it was expressed in books, inventions, or song—they found something outside themselves to use as a goal and a guide. Something that showed them a way to serve others, instead of living only for themselves.

Reading the stories of these courageous men and women not only helps us discover the principles that we will use to guide our own lives, but it teaches us about our black heritage and about America itself. It is crucial for us to know the heroes and heroines of our history and to realize that the price we paid in our struggle for equality in America was dear. But we must also understand that we have gotten as far as we have partly because America's democratic system and ideals made it possible.

We still are struggling with racism and prejudice. But the great men and women in this series are a tribute to the spirit of our democratic ideals and the system in which they have flourished. And that makes their stories special, and worth knowing. ☙

ELLA FITZGERALD

1

TWO STAGES

GLITTERING ON THE banks of the Potomac River in Washington, D.C., the John F. Kennedy Center was a particularly festive place on the night of December 2, 1979. Five prominent Americans were being honored inside the majestic theater for their lifetime achievements in the performing arts, and they were being saluted by a celebrity-filled audience, which included the wife of the president of the United States. Joining composer Aaron Copland, actor Henry Fonda, choreographer Martha Graham, and playwright Tennessee Williams as one of the honored guests was jazz legend Ella Fitzgerald. One of the world's best and most popular singers, she has long been regarded as the "First Lady of Song."

Hours before the ceremonies began at the Kennedy Center, Rosalynn Carter, the country's *real* first lady, had greeted the honored guests at a White House reception and had spoken of their contributions to the performing arts. "These five Americans are among the most talented who ever lived," said the wife of President Jimmy Carter. "They have given us insight, relaxation, joy and, above all, a deep awareness of our national heritage and our common humanity."

Thousands of dignitaries soon arrived at the Kennedy Center to echo Rosalynn Carter's sentiments and to take part in the gala celebration. The plush, red interior of the theater overflowed with rich and

Fitzgerald's tremendous vocal range and perfect pitch are among the many attributes that have helped her to remain an extremely popular vocalist for more than 50 years.

11

Along with Fitzgerald, four American artists received the distinguished Kennedy Center Honors in 1979: (from left to right) actor Henry Fonda, choreographer Martha Graham, playwright Tennessee Williams, and composer Aaron Copland. The festivities marked the second time ever that these honors were presented for a lifetime of achievements in the performing arts.

powerful figures from politics, society, and the world of entertainment. Then the five honorees entered the theater and sat alongside the first lady, in the first row of the balcony.

As the ceremonies began, a movie screen descended into view over the center of the stage. One by one, the life stories of the composer, the dancer, the actor, and the dramatist were told in short films shown on the giant screen. Finally, it was time for the singer's story to be told. Entertainer Peggy Lee, acting as a master of ceremonies, walked onto the stage and addressed the crowd. "Ella Fitzgerald is the greatest jazz singer of our time," she said, "the standard by which the rest of us are measured."

Then a segment of film clips that spanned Fitzgerald's career was shown. The clips chronicled her early success in the 1930s as well as her eventual

superstardom. A scene in which she did some playful scat singing, accompanied on the piano by bandleader and composer Duke Ellington, served to sum up her character. Her face in this scene was especially revealing. It radiated warmth, love, and respect.

As the brief film ended and the screen ascended until it disappeared from view, the audience arose in a thunderous ovation, paying homage to the 61-year-old singer. Fitzgerald, seated between Tennessee Williams and Aaron Copland, could not contain her emotions. Laughing and crying at the same time, she was overwhelmed, speechless with joy. It was all she could do to wave her handkerchief at the cheering crowd, to acknowledge their enthusiastic bravos and

Often called the "First Lady of Song," Fitzgerald was lauded by Rosalynn Carter, the first lady of the United States, shortly before the vocalist was honored at the Kennedy Center in the nation's capital on the night of December 2, 1979.

The Harlem Opera House was one of several theaters in New York City that began to hold amateur night contests in the early 1930s. The Harlem theater is shown here in 1934, when Fitzgerald, at the age of 16, made her first appearance onstage as a singer.

to thank them for their years of approval. She later said that it was "the proudest moment of my life."

When the roar died down, a trio of America's finest jazz singers—Joe Williams, Jon Hendricks, and Peggy Lee—took center stage. Backed by Count Basie and His Orchestra, they united their voices in a musical tribute to Fitzgerald. This was not the first tribute she had received, nor would it be the last. After nearly a half century as a performer, she had become a titan of jazz, inextricably linked to the music's growth, development, and continued popularity. According to radio personality Jonathan Schwartz, "The sound of her voice has been recorded more voluminously than the music made by any other single human being who ever lived, except for Bing Crosby." Even so Crosby himself admitted, "Man, woman or child, Ella is the greatest singer of them all."

Yet as Fitzgerald looked down from her balcony seat at the stage and the cheering Kennedy Center crowd in what may have been the crowning moment of her career, her thoughts must have drifted at least once, returning to another theater and audience from years past. The theater was the Harlem Opera House in the New York City district known as Harlem, and the year was 1934. The occasion was amateur night, with a terrified teenager named Ella waiting in the wings, nervously stealing peeks at the audience. To her, they seemed hungry for victims, ready to pounce. And she was to perform next.

Amateur nights in Harlem had begun the year before, at the Lafayette Theatre on 132nd Street, and had quickly become a staple of Harlem nightlife. The contests offered would-be singers, dancers, and comedians the chance to strut their stuff in the hopes of winning a prize, or maybe a crack at fame. Occasionally, a white contestant would try his or her luck. However, most of the performers on amateur night were black, and to many of them, success on the stage represented a possible way out of the economic depression that had been ravaging the country ever since the stock market crashed on October 24, 1929.

The effects of the Great Depression, which left many Americans homeless and unemployed, were particularly visible in Harlem. By 1930, nearly half of the 200,000 blacks who lived in the district were on unemployment relief. One way in which many of these Harlem residents attempted to forget their troubles was to take in the nightlife in the local theaters and clubs.

Amateur contests were among the most popular attractions at Harlem theaters. By 1934, the theaters were holding amateur contests during most nights of

Amateur night contests were initially held in Harlem at the Lafayette Theatre in 1933. While introducing hopeful performers to the entertainment world, the theater also presented a vast array of established black artists, including singer Bessie Smith, actor Stepin Fetchit, and dancer Bill "Bojangles" Robinson.

the week. By the 1950s, these contests had become a Harlem tradition. More than 15,000 contestants were showcased on Harlem stages, and such noted singers as Sarah Vaughan, James Brown, and the Isley Brothers got their start in show business after a successful amateur night performance.

Tough audiences were also a Harlem tradition. As critics, Harlem theatergoers were legendary, for they demanded the best from newcomers and seasoned pros alike. When they were not satisfied with someone's performance, they got rowdy and would boo and heckle as loudly as they might cheer. Jack Schiffman, whose father owned the celebrated Apollo Theater, said of the audiences, "If they dig you, you're okay. But if you turn them off, brother, watch out! The inhabitants of the Buzzard's Roost [the top balcony] can pick your carcass clean."

So it was a very particular crowd that 16-year-old Ella Fitzgerald knew she would face as she nervously shifted from foot to foot backstage at the Harlem Opera House, waiting to go on. What was she doing there? she wondered. She was not a performer. She was just a high school student from the suburb of

Amateur night at the Apollo Theater featured all kinds of entertainment, ranging from comedy to music to dance. Fitzgerald was planning on becoming a dancer rather than a singer when she went onstage for her very first appearance in a talent show.

Yonkers, New York. What was she doing on a stage in the big city, thinking that she could dance?

Yet there *was* a reason why Ella was taking part in an amateur contest. Maintaining that "everybody in Yonkers thought I was a good dancer," she hoped to dance professionally someday. She felt that her chance to make her mark had arrived after she had won a bet with two girlfriends. "We all wanted to get on the stage," she explained, "and we drew straws to see which of us would go on the amateur hour. I drew the short straw."

As Ella peeked once more at the audience, she tried not to think about her good fortune—or was it bad luck?—in drawing the short straw. Suddenly, she noticed with alarm that the act onstage—the act before *she* was supposed to go onstage—was also a dance act: two agile, acrobatic sisters, who commanded rousing applause as they finished. Once again, Ella wondered what had made an ungainly girl such as her think that she could dance?

By then, it was too late for Ella to bow out. The emcee had already announced her name and was calling her onto the stage, telling the crowd that she was going to dance for them. "My legs turned to water and a million butterflies played tag in my stomach," she said later. "They almost had to shove me onstage, and when I looked where I thought the audience should be, all I saw was a big blur."

The band started playing. Ella stared into the footlights, but nothing happened. Her limbs felt like rubber, then sand. She was too petrified to move. The audience started shifting in their seats and clearing their voices. The emcee whispered to her from offstage, "Tap . . . Do *something.*"

With her body failing her, Ella's mind started to race, trying to come up with something for her to do other than dance. She began to think about the music that she heard on the radio and on the records that her mother had around the house. Her thoughts set-

Like most of the top night spots in Harlem, the Apollo Theater attracted audiences that were very judgmental and quick to let popular artists know when they were not performing to the best of their abilities. Singer Billie Holiday said of her debut at the theater, "They didn't ask me what my style was, who I was. . . . They just [brought down] the house."

Fitzgerald mesmerized the audience during her first amateur night appearance with her rendition of "Judy," a song popularized by the Boswell Sisters (shown here). The audience responded to her performance with such excited applause that she then decided to pursue a singing career.

tled on her favorite singer, the sweet-voiced Connee Boswell, who performed swing numbers with her sisters. Ella liked to sing along with them whenever she heard one of their songs.

Softly, Ella started to sing one of the Boswell Sisters' tunes, entitled "Judy." The band, which knew the song, began to accompany her by playing the melody. Her voice gradually grew stronger and more confident as it relaxed into the song's easy, swinging rhythm. Before long, she could see smiles forming in the sea of dark faces in front of her.

When the song ended, the theater erupted into cheers. Shaking with fear but happy nonetheless, Ella stayed onstage and began another song popularized by the Boswell Sisters, "The Object of My Affection." This time, the crowd hung on her every note. She directed her voice at them as she moved her body in time to the music.

Immediately after Ella finished singing, the audience started to whistle and applaud, and the emcee announced that she had won a $25 prize. "It was the hardest money I ever earned," she admitted, acknowledging that she had won over what was perhaps the toughest audience in the world.

In the process, a star had been born. Calling this performance "the turning point of my life," Ella promptly decided to become a professional singer. "Once up there," she said, "I felt the acceptance and love from the audience—I knew I wanted to sing before people the rest of my life."

In the more than 50 years that have followed her first appearance onstage, Ella Fitzgerald has done just that. She has steadily grown as a performer—thanks to her versatility and determination, and to two people who believed in her talent: Chick Webb, the hunchbacked dwarf who hired her to sing with his band, and Norman Granz, the promoter who nurtured her career and helped to establish her as a major artist. Her career—which has traversed the liveliness of the big-band era, the period of frenzied dance-hall craziness known as swing, and the uncompromising, unconventional form of jazz called bebop—has flourished largely because of her mastery of different musical styles. According to *Ebony* magazine, "Her library of songs constitutes as thorough a record as is available anywhere of America's changing moods and emotions."

Representing the entire tradition of jazz, Fitzgerald has continually kept the fire in the music alive. Having performed with such jazz legends as Duke Ellington and trumpeter Louis Armstrong, she has become the guardian of their spirit and the keeper of the flame. For this reason, she has received many awards in addition to the $25 presented to her on amateur night and the honors bestowed on her at the Kennedy Center. An immensely talented artist, she has become, in the words of musician and jazz critic Leonard Feather, "one of the elite few for whom a single name on a marquee would suffice almost anywhere in the world." ∞

2

SINGING LESSONS

❧

ELLA FITZGERALD WAS born in Newport News, Virginia, on April 25, 1918, at a time when jazz was just beginning to develop into a distinct art form.

Several styles of black music—blues, spirituals, field hollers, African rhythms, folk songs, marches, and ragtime—all played a part in the evolution of jazz. In the early 1900s, various elements from these different musical styles were synthesized into jazz sounds in New Orleans, Louisiana. These sounds then spread to Kansas City, Missouri; Chicago, Illinois; and New York City, in styles that varied from city to city. By the early 1920s, jazz had become the first black art form to gain widespread acceptance. However, it is impossible to pinpoint exactly how this happened because jazz developed as it became mixed with other styles of music.

Just as the origins of jazz are uncertain, many facts about Ella's early life have been obscured by the time that has passed. When she was still quite young, she and her mother, Tempie, moved from Virginia to Yonkers, New York, becoming part of a mass migration in which millions of southern blacks headed northward in search of steady work and a better way of life. Ella never got to know her real father, who died shortly after World War I ended in 1918.

While Fitzgerald was growing up near the district of Harlem in New York City, racial segregation was a way of life even at the noted Cotton Club—one of several night spots in Harlem that employed black entertainers but did not admit black patrons.

21

The development of jazz music, which became the first art form originated by blacks to gain a large national audience, coincided with Fitzgerald's early years. The original jazz groups (including the one shown here) hailed from the South and were noted for playing improvised music.

An only child in a strange new town, Ella nevertheless did not suffer from any lack of love. "I had a warm family life," she said. "We had love and we had hope." In Yonkers, she and her mother lived with a man who was like a stepfather to Ella.

Yet life in the New York City suburb was often hard for Ella and her mother, who lived in a mixed neighborhood, with Italian, Spanish, and Portuguese neighbors. Her mother worked as a caterer and at a laundry while her "stepfather" was a ditchdigger and a chauffeur. "We didn't have much," Ella said. To help support her family, she accepted part-time jobs while she went to school.

During Ella's childhood in the early 1920s, the nearby island of Manhattan became a center of black artistic and intellectual life. By the middle of the decade, blacks from all over the country were migrating to the district of Harlem to take part in the spirited movement in literature and the arts that came to be known as the Harlem Renaissance. Among the leading figures in this period of black cultural achievement were poets Countee Cullen, Claude McKay, and Langston Hughes.

Entertainers as well as artists and writers displayed the creative spirit that characterized Harlem in the 1920s. Talented musicians such as Louis Armstrong, Fletcher Henderson, Fats Waller, and Duke Ellington became popular performers in Harlem's lively clubs and cabarets and helped to establish New York City as the nation's jazz capital. According to Ellington, Harlem in the 1920s was "just like the Arabian Nights" because its atmosphere was so exotic.

Yet Harlem, which soon became Ella's stomping ground, had a familiar look as well. Although the

Bandleader and composer Duke Ellington (in center, backed by his orchestra) was one of the more prominent musicians who helped to popularize jazz while Fitzgerald was growing up. In 1923, he arrived in New York City and began to refine his jazz sounds, contributing greatly to the black cultural movement in the 1920s that came to be known as the Harlem Renaissance.

After blacks from all over the country journeyed to Harlem in the 1920s to take part in the growing community, a number of well-to-do whites began to patronize the lively district, including heavyweight champion Jack Dempsey (center), shown here at a racially segregated nightclub called Connie's Inn.

district's many night spots—including Connie's Inn and the glamorous Cotton Club—featured black entertainers, some of these clubs were racially segregated and admitted only white patrons. Among the frequent customers at these exclusive clubs were wealthy whites and the biggest stars on Broadway. Bandleader Cab Calloway said, "Negroes from the Harlem community would line up outside to watch the limousines drive up—Cadillacs and Rolls-Royces and Duesenbergs long enough to make you choke—and the celebrities come and go."

The racial segregation that was practiced in these clubs had been legally sanctioned in the United States since the end of the Civil War, when Jim Crow laws

Fitzgerald was among the many theatergoers who flocked to Harlem in the early 1930s, when jazz was attracting new listeners by generating sounds and expressing moods that were not found in other forms of popular music.

calling for separate facilities for blacks and whites began to be passed. The Supreme Court reinforced these laws in 1896 when it ruled in the case of *Plessy vs. Ferguson* that segregation was legal so long as the separate facilities were basically equal in quality. Although this ruling was supposed to guarantee "separate but equal" conditions for blacks and whites, the separate facilities for blacks continued to be virtually inferior to the facilities reserved for whites. Racial discrimination thereby went under the guise of racial segregation.

When Ella was about 11 years old, she had her first encounter with racial prejudice: A boy at school directed a racial slur at her. Ella promptly pushed him down. "The other kids thought I had hit him—so I became a heroine at the school!" she said. "They made him apologize, and after that everyone looked up to me."

However, Ella was also learning by that time not to be so brazen. One day, she was walking home from junior high school with her mother after having appeared in a school play. Feeling a sense of superiority because of how well she had performed in the play, Ella ignored a fellow student who had come over to talk to her. Ella's mother promptly gave her daughter a slap. According to Ella, "She said, 'Don't you ever go around where you don't speak to somebody, because someday that might be the very person who could be in a position to help you.' That's something I've always kept in mind."

Besides teaching humility to Ella, her mother helped to sharpen Ella's musical sense. "To have be-

Prior to becoming a top bandleader in the mid-1930s, William "Count" Basie was a pianist with the Bennie Moten Orchestra, one of the first bands in the country to play a style of jazz known as swing.

come who I am and what I am has been because of people helping me through the years," Ella admitted. "Not just those buying records, but good friends, good family. There's always got to be somebody there to help." Tempie played records, sang around the house, and spent a fair amount of her hard-earned money on a piano teacher for her daughter. "I was so fascinated listening to him talk and play that I hardly learned a thing," Ella said. She also studied music at school and sang in the glee club.

On weekends, Ella and her friends would tap dance in public for money. The enthusiasm that other people showed for her dancing eventually encouraged her to enter an amateur contest at the Harlem Opera House. She not only won the contest (although it was for her singing rather than for her dancing) when she was 16 years old, but she won contests for her singing at the Apollo Theater and other theaters as well. Performing "Believe It, Beloved" in addition to two songs popularized by the Boswell Sisters, she began to develop a reputation as a singer who was a crowd pleaser.

Although Ella had little difficulty in charming the audiences, her leap to great success did not happen overnight. The development of her singing career was delayed by a number of false starts. One of these false starts occurred in 1934, after saxophonist Benny Carter had been bowled over by Ella during one of her amateur night performances.

The saxophonist introduced Ella to John Hammond, a well-regarded record producer who helped to establish the careers of a number of important jazz artists, including singer Billie Holiday and bandleader Count Basie. Carter and Hammond invited her to sing for Fletcher Henderson, the bandleader of one of the country's top orchestras, but he was not very impressed by her. "He said, 'Don't call me, I'll call you,'" Ella stated.

Like Fitzgerald, singer Billie Holiday spent the early years of her singing career performing in Harlem night spots. At the age of 17 she was discovered by record producer John Hammond, who soon tried to help Fitzgerald establish a singing career as well.

Also in 1934, talent scouts at the Columbia Broadcasting System (CBS) got wind of Ella's vocal abilities and considered putting her on a radio show called "The Street Singer." The star of the program was popular radio entertainer Arthur Tracy. Ella auditioned for the show and was offered a contract. But then tragedy struck: Her mother died suddenly, turning Ella into an orphaned minor without a legal guardian. Because she did not have anyone to take over the legal responsibility of her contract, the deal had to be called off.

For a while, Ella lived in Yonkers with her mother's sister, Virginia Williams. She also lived at an orphanage. Yet the change in her home life did not stop her from continuing to visit Harlem for the amateur night contests.

A contest at the Lafayette Theatre proved to be one of the few low points in her career. During her turn in the spotlight, she tried to break in a new

In the early 1920s, Fletcher Henderson (left) became the first bandleader to divide a big band into different musical instrument sections. This novel arrangement enabled his band to fuse dance orchestra music with the sounds of jazz and ultimately led to the development of swing.

song, entitled "Lost in a Fog." However, the pianist did not play the right chords, which caused Ella to lose her place in the song. The audience responded by booing her off the stage.

Ella refused to let this setback stop her. "People always assume you started in the church or you just got a lucky break," she said, "but it isn't where you came from, it's where you're going that counts, and how your attitude is, and not getting discouraged." She returned to the Harlem Opera House, and she was rewarded for her singing with the offer of a professional engagement. To enable this engagement to take place, two years were added to her birth date so that she would no longer be considered a minor.

During the Great Depression, dining and dancing remained a popular form of nightly entertainment in Harlem as many of the district's residents frequented local night spots in an attempt to forget about their troubled times.

Fitzgerald made her first professional appearance—as a featured singer with Tiny Bradshaw's band—on February 15, 1935. An advertisement for the week-long engagement at the Harlem Opera House is shown here.

In February 1935, Ella made her first professional appearance as part of a show that featured Tiny Bradshaw's band. It turned out to be a weeklong engagement, for which she earned $50. She said, "They put me on right at the end, when everybody had on their coats and was getting ready to leave. Tiny said, 'Ladies and gentlemen, here is the young girl that's been winning all the contests,' and they all came back and took their coats off and sat back down again."

It was most likely during one of these appearances that Ella was spotted by Bardou Ali, the master of ceremonies for the Chick Webb Orchestra, one of the top bands in New York City. Ali, who responded immediately to Ella's voice, thought that her clear tone and impeccable sense of rhythm would nicely suit the percussive drive of Webb's band. The problem was: How to convince his boss that she belonged in the group?

3

DISCOVERED!

By THE TIME Ella was preparing to audition for Chick Webb's band in 1935, most jazz bands were playing a style of music that was quickly becoming a national phenomenon. The music was called swing because it was full of high spirits and emphasized lively rhythms. Making use of a steadily accented beat, it was designed especially to encourage dancing.

Some people objected to swing on moral grounds, convinced that its hot, throbbing rhythms could only lead to loose behavior or to wild and dangerous passion. But most listeners did not take such complaints seriously; they were too busy enjoying themselves. For swing was party music, perfect for dancing and good times, and the large orchestras that played the spirited sounds of swing helped people to forget about the dire effects of the Great Depression.

A band was said to swing successfully when the interaction of its members resulted in music that sounded instinctively correct. The large swing orchestras of the 1930s featured soloists—just as the orchestras did in the 1920s. However, the popularity of each swing band rested on how well its members played together.

The most successful swing bands made use of arrangers who could take a song and divide its parts among the various instruments. When two bands

Fitzgerald was barely 17 years old when she joined the Chick Webb Orchestra during the lively swing era. She was groomed as a vocalist by bandleader Chick Webb, who limited her to uptempo songs until she gained more singing experience.

33

played different arrangements of the same song, they usually played the song in completely distinct ways. Consequently, unique arrangements not only enabled the players in a band to work in swinging combinations that would catch and hold the public's attention, but such arrangements also allowed a band to develop a trademark sound. "The big bands were like big league ball teams," jazz critic George T. Simon said, "and the kids knew all the players—even without a scorecard."

Like New Orleans–style jazz, swing was developed by black musicians. However, these musicians did not achieve the same widespread popularity that was enjoyed by the white musicians who began to play swing in the mid-1930s. As had happened in the early days of jazz, white listeners favored white groups over black ones. The most popular white swing bands were the orchestras led by Jimmy and Tommy Dorsey, clarinetist Artie Shaw, and clarinetist Benny Goodman, who became known as the "King of Swing."

By the 1930s, Duke Ellington (center) had become the leader of the most popular black jazz band in the country. An extremely productive composer, he was also acclaimed for his ability to blend the talents of musicians who possessed different musical styles.

The racial barriers that kept many white jazz fans from listening to black musicians started to break down once Goodman began to hire black arrangers as well as black sidemen to play with his white musicians. Among the people whom he hired was Fletcher Henderson, whose arrangements contributed greatly to the success of the Benny Goodman Orchestra. Goodman's actions ultimately encouraged many of his white fans to listen to black swing orchestras and thereby helped the bands of Duke Ellington, Count Basie, and Chick Webb become all the more popular.

Born in Baltimore, Maryland, in 1909, William Henry Webb, Jr., was nicknamed "Chick" because he was so small. When he was a child, he contracted tuberculosis of the spine; and when he fell down a flight of stairs, the combination of his illness and the effects of the fall left him partially paralyzed in his legs. He grew up to be a hunchbacked dwarf who stood just over four feet tall. Nevertheless, he proved to be indomitable.

Clarinetist Benny Goodman (right) was the first white band-leader to hire and feature black musicians. Formed in 1934, his orchestra soon became the most popular band of the swing era.

When Webb was still a boy, his doctors suggested that he start drumming as therapy for his stiffened limbs. Sticks in hand, he began to bang on everything that he could find around the house, including cans, pots, and pans. He then peddled newspapers so he could buy himself a real drum kit. He later boasted that he sold 3,000 papers in one day.

The same drive that Webb displayed as a paperboy brought him to New York City in 1924, eager for work as a drummer. Duke Ellington recognized his natural ability and got him his first job in the city, playing at the Black Bottom Club. There he began to jam alongside Harlem's finest musicians, listening to them and learning. Before long, he had begun recruiting them for a band.

By the time that Webb was 17 years old, he was leading his own band, which specialized in dance music. Jazz orchestras in the 1920s usually featured a large number of musicians playing a style of music that combined jazz rhythms and improvised solos with the sounds of dance orchestra music. Webb's ear for talent was so good that Ellington, Fletcher Henderson, and other bandleaders started hiring musicians away from him for their own bands.

By 1933, Webb had built up the reputation of his band to the point where it played regularly at the Savoy, one of the most popular ballrooms in Harlem. The music that Webb's band played was like its leader's personality: upbeat and good-natured, full of energy and life. Tenor saxophonist Teddy McRae said, "He could make you play whether you felt like it or not. You could come to work tired, he'd make you feel good."

By then, Webb had already become known as a great dance drummer. He was, according to celebrated drummer Gene Krupa, "the most luminous of all drum stars, the master," which was ironic because Webb's own legs could not dance and he could barely reach the bass drum pedal. Yet his wrists and ankles were very strong, and he used them to keep the big beat going. In spite of his handicaps, he was determined to be the best at everything he did.

The one thing greater than Webb's talent was his heart. No sacrifice was too great if it meant making his band better or helping out his musicians. He would forgo food to buy music for the band; he would pay the bills when another musician was hospitalized with tuberculosis. "If a sideman left him, even without notice," trumpeter Taft Jordan said, "Chick would take him back whenever the guy needed work."

In order for Ella to win a job with the band, she and Bardou Ali first had to come up with a plan that would appeal to Webb's heart. He was not very interested in having Ella join the band because he thought that the public was more eager to hear hot arrangements—the different ways in which a band could

Noted for his lively jazz shows, drummer Chick Webb won over most audiences with his energetic performances. Fellow drummer Sam Woodyard said of him, "He knew how to shade and color, and how to bring a band up and keep it there."

In 1935, Fitzgerald joined male vocalist Charlie Linton (left) as a singer in the Chick Webb Orchestra. Within a few years, she emerged as the group's lead singer.

divide a song among the instrumentalists—than a vocalist. Besides, the band already had a singer, a male vocalist named Charlie Linton.

One night in 1935, Ali snuck the 17-year-old singer into Webb's dressing room while the band was onstage at a Harlem theater. When Webb returned to his dressing room during the intermission and found the two waiting for him, he realized that he had no choice but to listen to Ella perform the songs that she always sang on amateur nights. He listened closely, keeping in mind the school prom that the band was scheduled to play on the following day in New Haven, Connecticut.

The room became quiet after Ella had finished. Then Webb said, "We'll take her to Yale tomorrow, and if she goes over with the college kids, she stays." The next afternoon, she traveled with the band to New Haven and nervously strolled across the Yale campus, hoping that this audition would be the last one she would ever have to give.

For her debut with the band, Ella wore a gown that Bradshaw and some chorus girls had bought for her. Moe Gale, Webb's manager and part owner of the Savoy, was one of several people who were concerned about her less than glamorous appearance. Yet

Moe Gale (left) was one of several people to influence Fitzgerald's career. He not only owned the Savoy Ballroom, one of Harlem's premier showcases, but also managed Chick Webb (right) and his band.

Fitzgerald and a smiling Chick Webb (left), her legal guardian, exhibit their special chemistry during a performance by his orchestra at the Savoy.

he and the others need not have worried. As Ella sang for the students and heard their enthusiastic applause filling the hall, it became obvious that she had won a steady job with the band. In a week, she would be singing at the Savoy—the hippest, grandest dance spot in Harlem.

However, a pressing problem still had to be worked out: Being an orphan, Ella did not have a legal guardian. Webb, at the age of 26, and his wife, Sallye, agreed to adopt the teenager and become her legal guardians, then gave her the necessary permission to join the band. In giving her a home as well as a job, they not only helped to start her career but demonstrated faith in her talent and provided her with friendship.

In time, Ella's musical association with Webb would be so harmonious and seem so right that different stories would circulate about how he had discovered her. Many accounts said that he saw her on amateur night and rushed backstage to sign her. But the truth was that he had to be persuaded to hear her sing. "I always thought my music was pretty much hollering," she said, "but he didn't." Once he heard her, he was convinced. "There was so much music in the man," Ella explained. ❧

4

STOMPING AT THE SAVOY

CLUBS AND BALLROOMS prospered in New York City, Ella's hometown, during the swing era. The downtown section housed such night spots as the Paramount, the Capitol, and Roseland; uptown were Small's Paradise, the Cotton Club, and the Apollo. However, during swing's peak years, the most popular Harlem nightclub was the Savoy.

Opened for business on March 6, 1926, the Savoy was soon advertised as "The World's Most Famous Ballroom." Located on the second floor of a block-long building on Lenox Avenue between 140th and 141st streets, the club had a reputation for being safe (well-dressed bouncers protected the female patrons from troublemakers) and well run. Unlike some other clubs in Harlem, the Savoy admitted people from all races and classes. Ella went to the club to socialize long before she started to sing there professionally.

The Savoy's big ballroom featured a stage that could disappear from view and two bandstands upon which orchestras would alternate sets. When one of the orchestras would finish its set, the other one would immediately begin to play. If an orchestra could not entice people onto the dance floor, it was not invited back to the club.

The ballroom was nicknamed "the Track" partly because it looked like a racecourse and partly because the dancers' shoes left track marks on the floor. The

"To hear her," one writer said of Fitzgerald, "is to be given, in the most telling and pleasurable form, that particular lift of the spirits that is the great gift of jazz."

43

Harlem's most popular night spot during the swing era, the Savoy was as much a dance hall as it was a music showcase. After opening in 1926, the ballroom remained in operation for more than 30 years.

dance area was the largest in Harlem. It measured 50 feet by 200 feet and bounced slightly whenever it was supporting a gyrating crowd. The dancers at the Savoy were all wildly enthusiastic, as if dancing at the club was their life's occupation. Many of them came every night and danced into the wee hours of the morning.

Patrons of the club did dances named the Jitterbug, the Congeroo, and the Suzy Q. But the most famous dance at the Savoy was the Lindy Hop, inspired by aviator Charles Lindbergh's heroic solo flight from New York to Paris in 1927. To do the Lindy Hop, a male dancer would toss his partner in the air, with her legs kicking, and then he would drag her along the floor and slide her feetfirst through his arched legs. The movements of the dance imitated—and celebrated—Lindbergh's takeoff and landing.

Lindy Hoppers considered Webb to be a superior dance drummer. Consequently, his orchestra played regularly at the Savoy as the unofficial house band, and they always did their best to rock the house whenever they played. Webb paid a lasting tribute to the club in 1934 when he recorded "Stomping at the Savoy," a song by Edgar Sampson, one of his arrangers. The song soon became a big-band standard.

The first record that Ella made with the Chick Webb Orchestra, a song called "Love and Kisses," was cut on June 12, 1935. Shortly after the band made this record, it was on tour in Philadelphia, Pennsylvania. One night on the tour, Ella went with some of the band members to a night spot where the song was listed on the jukebox. However, she was not allowed inside because she was underage. "So I had some fellow who was over 21 go in and put a

Fitzgerald and Charlie Linton share the vocals during a set by the Chick Webb Orchestra.

Fitzgerald recorded several hits with Chick Webb (left) during their four-year-long association. Yet she was not allowed to enter certain establishments and listen to her first record on the jukebox because she was still a minor.

nickel in," she said, "while I stood outside and listened to my own voice coming out."

Twenty-minute versions of songs such as "Stardust," which had become popular in a much briefer version, were the band's specialty at the Savoy. Part of the band would start at a medium-speed tempo and maintain it while others joined in, playing claves, maracas, and other percussive instruments. By then, the whole band would be rocking, and the ballroom floor would be shaking from all of the energetic activity.

When Ella joined the Chick Webb Orchestra in 1935, she was eased in slowly at the Savoy. Believing that she was not quite ready to perform ballads, Webb restricted her singing to uptempo numbers, reminding her to follow the beat. Many people in the crowd were about the same age as the 17-year-old singer, and they took to her immediately. And she felt right at home with them. "Between songs, when I wasn't singing, instead of being on the bandstand, I'd be out on the floor, dancing," she said.

But the Savoy was not only known for its dancing. Featuring two bandstands, the club was also celebrated for its battles of the bands. Good-natured yet hotly competitive, these musical face-offs between two opposing bands quickly became a club tradition.

During these battles, the dueling orchestras would alternate sets. As they would play songs back and

A newcomer to the jazz scene, Fitzgerald shares a light moment with Count Basie between sets at the Savoy.

forth into the night, each song would get louder and rougher. Because the Chick Webb Orchestra was the house band at the Savoy, they were often asked to defend their "turf" against visiting bands. The audience decided the victor in these battles, and Ella's singing during these contests helped her to win many new fans.

Webb and his musicians loved to battle. They would play softly and unaggressively at first, lulling the members of the rival band into thinking that Webb's orchestra would not prove to be very stiff competition. Then all of a sudden, Webb and his musicians would turn the battle around and overwhelm the other band. They would win easily against such prominent groups as Joe "King" Oliver's band, the Casa Loma Orchestra, and Erskine Hawkins's orchestra.

Occasionally, another orchestra would steal Webb's thunder at the Savoy and outplay his musicians. Such was the case when they faced Duke Ellington and His Orchestra, the most popular band in the entire country. Before the contest began, Webb boasted to his

Bandleader Duke Ellington entertains Fitzgerald and vocalist Ivie Anderson at the Savoy, where he and his orchestra became one of the few groups to defeat the Chick Webb Orchestra in a battle of the bands.

tenor saxophonist Teddy McRae that they were "gonna make this cat work tonight." Yet Ellington did not see the need for the two bands to battle. "Look man," he told Webb, "we got the place full, we aint gettin' no more money, why knock our brains out?"

But Webb would not give in; he insisted on having a battle. So when Ellington's band finished its set, Webb's orchestra immediately started another set in which the music was faster and wilder than before. People began to shout for Ellington's band to fight back. With so much encouragement, Ellington and his musicians started to perform again, playing so hard and loud that their music eventually caused several windows in the club to give way. At that point, Webb conceded defeat.

Yet a shining hour at the Savoy was soon to come for Webb—and for Ella as well. On May 11, 1937, the members of the Chick Webb Orchestra became involved in their wildest and most dramatic battle, playing against the members of the Benny Goodman Orchestra. The battle marked the first performance ever given in Harlem by the "King of Swing."

Before the battle began, Goodman was anxious to hear Webb's orchestra, and so he visited the Savoy with the hopes of hearing them rehearse. However, Webb and his musicians had a plan of their own. When Goodman showed up, they sought to fool him by changing the tempo of their songs so that they did not sound like they usually did. Webb's musicians restored the right tempo to the music during their rehearsal on the night of the battle.

The scene at the Savoy on that night was pandemonium. By midnight, the club was filled with 4,000 fans, and another 5,000 were lining the streets outside, causing traffic to come to a halt. The riot squad, the fire department, and the police tried to keep the crowd under control and to prevent them from rushing into the club. Inside the Savoy, five

On the night of May 11, 1937, "King of Swing" Benny Goodman (left) and band member Gene Krupa (right) provided one of the most exciting battles of the bands ever held at the Savoy. Chick Webb, according to one account, "finished the session with a drum solo, winning a thunderous ovation, while Goodman and his drummer, Gene Krupa, just stood there shaking their heads."

policemen stood guard on the stage to prevent the audience from pressing too close to the musicians.

Shortly before the show began, Webb spoke to Ella and the other musicians. "This is the turning point of this band," he said. "You know how much this means to me."

Goodman's band started the battle and caused the audience to send up a roar. Next came Webb and his band, who were greeted by cheers from the club's regulars. When one band finished, the other one began to play. The music continued to grow louder and hotter.

By the time Webb and his orchestra launched into an instrumental called "Harlem Congo," it was clear that they were winning the battle. Then Ella took her place by the microphone, at the center of the bandstand. As she started to sing, the crowd locked arms and swayed back and forth in time to the sound of her voice. Even before she ended her performance, it was clear that Goodman and his band had lost the battle. Thanks in part to Ella's efforts, the "King of Swing" had been dethroned.

Following such powerful performances, Ella's reputation began to grow. It continued to increase even more when she made appearances with the band on "remote" radio broadcasts. Through the 1920s and 1930s, jazz recordings were rarely played over the radio. Instead, the radio carried nightly broadcasts from the ballrooms and clubs.

Ella's wide vocal range (about $2\frac{1}{2}$ octaves) and her impeccable sense of pitch, harmony, and rhythm all contributed greatly to her rising success. Her voice, according to *Ebony*, "contains as many tonal shades as colors in the spectrum." Almost instinctively, she would seek out the right note, the correct beat, and the precise amount of tonal coloring. She showed the ability to take a song and sing it in a straightforward manner, or turn it around and mix it up without batting an eye.

Nightly radio broadcasts from the Savoy helped Fitzgerald to build up a large following in the late 1930s.

Louis Armstrong is generally credited with inventing jazz vocals, originating this type of singing in the 1920s. Although other women sang jazz before Ella did, she was the first female vocalist to establish a unique, jazz-like style. By the time she won the *Down Beat* magazine poll as the top female vocalist in 1937, her importance to the world of jazz—and to Webb's band—had become clear. Her singing was bringing the band more attention than they would ever have received on their own. Music publishers started offering their best new songs, which they ordinarily saved for the better-known white vocalists, to Webb for Ella to record. "This is it," Webb said, "I have a real singer now. That's what the public wants."

As her popularity grew with the Chick Webb Orchestra, Fitzgerald made her first Broadway appearance, at New York City's Paramount Theater.

To please Ella's fans, Webb decided to feature her on the band's jazz records. Yet it was a novelty song, recorded in 1938, that ultimately made her a star. The song was conceived by her while the band was on tour in Boston, Massachusetts, shortly after Webb had checked into a local hospital.

Ella sat down at a piano and began to fiddle with the keys. Searching to come up with a song that would cheer up Webb, she thought back to the time when she was a little girl who used to play a game with her friends called "Drop the Handkerchief." Part of the game included a rhyme that went "A-tisket, a-tasket, a green and yellow basket." While saying these words out loud, she picked out notes to accompany them. Later on, she told Al Feldman, one of Webb's arrangers, "I got something terrific! They're swinging everything else—why not nursery rhymes?"

The result of Ella and Feldman's collaboration was "A-Tisket, A-Tasket." The band recorded the song—described as a "jitterbug spiritual"—in May 1938, and it became a smash as soon as it was released. Fitting right in with "My Wubba Dolly," "The Flat Foot Floogie with the Floy Floy," and other silly swing tunes that were then popular, it topped the song charts for 17 weeks and became one of the biggest records of the decade. Suddenly, girls everywhere were singing along with the record and trying to imitate Ella's vocal style.

Ella's rise to fame tested her loyalty. Bandleader Jimmy Lunceford tried to hire her for his band at the rate of $75 a week, but she refused to leave Webb, who was not only her boss but part of her family. In return for staying with the band, she was given a raise.

During this period, Ella strayed from the band only once, when she married a recent acquaintance named Benny Kornegay on a dare. "The guys in the band were all crying when I told them," she said.

At the age of 23, Fitzgerald married dancer Benny Kornegay. She is shown here leaving a courthouse after the marriage was annulled almost one year later.

During the 1930s, Fitzgerald and the Chick Webb Orchestra broke several racial barriers. She is shown here with the orchestra in 1939, when it became the first black band to play at the exclusive Park Central Hotel in New York City.

They had the marriage quickly annulled by a judge, who told Ella, "You just keep singing 'A-Tisket, A-Tasket' and leave those men alone."

With Ella helping Webb's orchestra to reach its peak in popularity, they began to break some new ground. They became the first jazz band to play at Levaggi's, a prominent Boston restaurant, and the first black band to be featured at New York City's Park Central Hotel. They also headlined on Broadway at the Paramount Theater, an engagement indicating that the band had become a success with white audiences. During that engagement, members of the audience jumped from their seats to touch Ella and to shake her hand. At one show, some people in the audience even ripped her gown in their enthusiasm.

Success kept the band working nonstop, and all of the work soon grew to be too much for Webb. Even though he had a great amount of stamina, his crippled body was not strong enough to cope with the pressures of stardom. By 1939, he was hardly strong enough to finish a set. Sometimes, he would faint after performing. Yet he would never admit to being sick out of fear of letting down his musicians. He would tell them, "I'm gonna be so well in another couple of months. Besides, I've gotta keep my guys working."

But illness finally caught up with Webb later that year, while the band was beginning a tour of the

Chick Webb's widow, Sallye (center), is comforted by Fitzgerald and a nurse during funeral services for the popular bandleader at the Waters African Methodist Church in Baltimore, Maryland.

Thousands of mourners pay their final respects to Chick Webb as his funeral, held on June 20, 1939, draws to a close.

South. Their opening date was on a riverboat in Washington, D.C. After the show, Webb announced to the band that he was going to the Johns Hopkins Medical Center in his hometown of Baltimore, for a checkup before the tour was fully under way. Once he was at the hospital, the doctors discovered that he had pneumonia and was simply too frail to treat.

On the night of June 16, 1939, as relatives gathered around his bed, Webb asked his mother to lift him up. He smiled at her and said, "Sorry, I gotta go," and then died. He was barely 30 years old.

Webb's band, which was playing in Montgomery, Alabama, when the news of his death was announced, traveled to Baltimore for the funeral. It proved to be one of the largest ever held in the city, with 80 cars in the procession and thousands of mourners crowding the streets and rooftops. As a final tribute to her friend, Ella sang a song called "My Buddy" over his casket.

Ella's guardian and mentor, Webb had cared for her and provided her with musical training. After she had made a name for herself, he had shaped his band around her, acknowledging that her talent had eclipsed his own. They had been opposites in some ways: He was outgoing and diminutive, she was big and shy. Yet they had been musical soulmates, as close to one another as if they were a real-life father and daughter.

Although Ella, at the age of 21, was once more on her own in life, Webb's guiding spirit continued to be with her. As a symbol of their bond, he had once given her a ring. "I thought it was something he wanted me to try on for size for his wife," she said, "but he said it was for me." ❧

5

VOCAL VARIATIONS

Cᴴ HICK WEBB'S DEATH in 1939 cast the future of his band in doubt. "I felt like quitting," Ella Fitzgerald said, "[but] the fact that people like me and I like people . . . kept me going." Webb's manager, Moe Gale, also decided that the band should go on just as it had before Webb's death, only now it should bear the name of its star vocalist: Ella Fitzgerald and Her Orchestra. He circulated a statement that read: "In accordance with Mr. Webb's wishes, Miss Fitzgerald has succeeded to the leadership of the band." The drum kit, which used to occupy center stage, was pushed to the background.

Barely 21 years old, Fitzgerald was suddenly one of the youngest bandleaders in the country. She was also one of the few women to be a bandleader. However, she was actually the bandleader in name only; a number of Webb's musicians in fact directed the band. Fitzgerald had become the frontperson simply because she was the best known member of the band. "They let me conduct one number each show," she said, "to make me feel like I was the leader."

For a while, the arrangement proved to be a satisfactory one as the orchestra played to good-sized crowds anxious to hear Fitzgerald sing. By September 1940, the band had traveled close to 20,000 miles

Fitzgerald took over the leadership (although it was basically in title only) of the Chick Webb Orchestra after her guardian's death in 1939.

59

and had toured across most of the United States. The band's main attraction was Fitzgerald, who in 1940 became the youngest person ever to join the American Society of Composers, Authors, and Publishers (ASCAP). In some places, her fans caused so much commotion that the police had to be summoned.

Despite the band's initial success, Ella Fitzgerald and Her Orchestra ran out of steam two years after it was established. Webb had been the glue that had held the unit together more than anyone could have guessed. Without his energy and exuberance, the band members lost interest in playing with one another and decided to disband.

Other factors also played a part in the orchestra's breakup and signaled the end of the big-band era. On December 7, 1941, the United States entered World War II, prompting the federal government to issue a number of regulations that affected most of its citizens. Tens of thousands of people from all over the country—including singers, musicians, and band-

Shortly after the band was organized in 1939, Ella Fitzgerald and Her Orchestra became a popular attraction throughout the country.

leaders—joined the armed forces. Gasoline, which had to be conserved for the war effort, was rationed, thereby making it difficult for large orchestras to travel and for fans to attend the shows. The imposition of curfews and amusement taxes made audiences less willing to go out for an evening of entertainment.

Perhaps the biggest blow of all to the big bands was a strike by the American Federation of Musicians (AFM) in 1942. A powerful union, the AFM got into a dispute with record companies and declared a ban on all recording. Due to this ban, no records were made for more than two years. Without sufficient exposure, many bands had to break up.

As sentimental songs and ballads became more popular in the early 1940s, individual singers began to overshadow the rest of the performers in the big bands. One of the best-known vocalists to emerge from the swing era was Frank Sinatra (left).

In the early 1940s, the public's tastes also shifted in the charged atmosphere of wartime. Sentimental songs grew in popularity as soldiers were sent overseas, forcing apart families and lovers throughout the country. Listeners began to identify with melancholy ballads and lyrics about love and parting instead of the lively sounds of the big bands.

As vocalists moved more and more into the limelight, Fitzgerald's reputation grew, and increased fame brought her new opportunities. In 1942, she went to Hollywood, California, to appear in her first film, *Ride 'Em Cowboy*, a comedy starring Bud Abbott and Lou Costello. She also continued to give concerts and write music and lyrics, helping to compose such songs as "You Showed Me the Way," "Oh, But I Do," and "Please Tell the Truth."

Fitzgerald first sang without the backing of a big band in 1942, when she appeared with the Four Keys quartet.

In September 1942, Fitzgerald made her first appearance with a small group, the Four Keys, at the Aquarium restaurant in New York City's Times Square. The public address system broke down, and she had to sing without amplification. Yet as soon as she started to sing, the noisy room became completely still. "What more can be said of any singer?" reported *Variety*, the entertainment industry's leading newspaper.

When Fitzgerald resumed making records, she was pleased to perform the latest style of music—sad ballads and popular songs. But she also made several efforts to expand her musical range. "A lot of singers think all they have to do is exercise their tonsils to get ahead," she said. "They refuse to look for new ideas and new outlets, so they fall by the wayside. . . . I'm going to try to find out the new ideas before the others do."

Fitzgerald's first musical experiment in the mid-1940s was with calypso—West Indian folk music featuring lyrics that are half-spoken and half-sung. Although she was warned that the country was not ready to accept calypso music, she went ahead with the experiment. "I got tired of singing about long lost loves," she said, "so when I came across a number called 'Stone Cold Dead in the Market,' I asked . . . if I could record it."

A novelty song, "Stone Cold Dead in the Market" tells the story of a woman who strikes her good-for-nothing husband with a frying pan. The humorous lyrics helped people accept the song's foreign-sounding music, and "Stone Cold Dead in the Market" wound up selling millions of copies. During one of Fitzgerald's concerts in Philadelphia, the audience made her sing it three times before they let her continue with the rest of her show.

Fitzgerald's most ambitious attempt to broaden her musical abilities occurred when she went back to singing jazz and tackled the difficult and controversial

During World War II, Fitzgerald not only made records, appeared in films, and sang in public but also performed for U.S. servicemen around the world.

style of music known as bebop. Originating in the early 1940s—a time when jazz was attracting smaller audiences than in previous years—bebop not only evolved from swing but, according to the jazz musicians in New York City who invented it, had surpassed swing. Among the first musicians to play bebop were pianist Thelonious Monk, drummer Kenny Clarke, and, more importantly, saxophonist Charlie Parker and trumpeter Dizzy Gillespie.

Bebop was almost the complete opposite of swing. It was usually played by small groups instead of big bands and was performed at jam sessions in small clubs instead of in large ballrooms. It was improvised rather than orchestrated and featured solos over ensemble playing.

Most of all, bebop was for listening rather than dancing. It was serious and subtle, not lighthearted and loud. With its strange altered chords and rhythmic variations, bebop challenged its listeners and was not very popular at first because it sounded odd to most people. A radio station in Los Angeles, California, even banned it from the airwaves.

Yet bebop was most definitely jazz. If anything, it represented an attempt by jazz musicians to go forward and break away from the restrictions that swing had put on soloists. According to music historian Dan Morgenstern, "In bebop, for the first time, jazz became music played for its own sake."

Gillespie, who had briefly played with Fitzgerald's orchestra in 1943, asked her to join his band for a six-week tour in 1947. After a career in swing, she could hear how jazz was changing, and she wanted to be a part of its growth, no matter what her fans might think. "Bop musicians have more to say than any other musicians playing today," she said. "They know what they're doing. . . . I've been inspired by them and I want the whole world to know it." Without a second thought, she accepted the opportunity to work with the man who cultivated a curious style of dress to match his innovative music. Gillespie generally wore a beret, a goatee, thick black horn-rimmed glasses, and a brightly colored tie.

Fitzgerald adapted her voice to the new jazz form by using a vocal style called scat singing. A vocalist "scats" when he or she abandons the lyrics of a song and uses nonsense syllables to carry the rhythm or express emotion just like an instrument does. Trumpeter Louis Armstrong is said to have originated scat singing. While he was recording what would become his first hit song, "Heebie Jeebies," in 1926, he accidentally dropped his sheet music. Instead of stopping the recording process to pick up the sheets, he

Saxophonist Charlie Parker helped to forge the style of jazz that came to be known as bebop. His innovative approach to rhythm and harmony has influenced virtually all subsequent jazz musicians.

Fitzgerald makes a record with saxophonist Louis Jordan in 1947 during the rise of bebop. She won over many new fans by introducing an unusual form of vocals— scat singing—into her musical repertoire.

kept on singing in his gravel voice, making up nonsense sounds to replace the actual lyrics as he sang.

Fitzgerald had tried scat singing earlier in her career, with the Chick Webb Orchestra. "We used to have nightly jam sessions in which all the musicians would improvise on their instruments," she said. "I felt out of place until Chick suggested I improvise on my voice."

But it was not until Fitzgerald toured with Gillespie and was exposed to his brand of bebop that she discovered the heights to which her scatting could soar. "Listening to Dizzy made me want to try something with my voice that would be like a horn," she said. "He'd shout 'Go ahead and blow' and I'd improvise." With her natural sense of pitch and rhythm, she caught on right away to the nuances of making her singing sound like bebop.

Before long, Fitzgerald began to put her version of bebop on records. In March 1947, she scatted

George and Ira Gershwin's "Oh Lady Be Good"; in December of the same year, she recorded "How High the Moon." Both recordings immediately became hits. Something new and unexpected, her scat singing delighted her listeners.

Fitzgerald was delighted by her scat singing as well. "They were honest-to-goodness 'jazz' records," she said in her enthusiasm for improvisation. "A jazz performance, by definition, is the spontaneous expression of an artist's emotion at the time of performance, not a rehearsed song, read from sheet music, devoid of creativity."

Fitzgerald's crowning achievement with bebop also came in 1947, when she and Gillespie headlined a sold-out concert at prestigious Carnegie Hall in New York City. "After that Carnegie Hall concert," Gil-

By the late 1940s, Harlem was no longer the popular center of black entertainment that it had been in previous decades. Only a few night spots—including Small's Paradise (shown here)—offered entertainment on a regular basis.

Trumpeter Dizzy Gillespie played a key role in Fitzgerald's development as a jazz singer by encouraging her to use her voice as a musical instrument.

lespie said, "everybody started paying attention to the music." Because Fitzgerald was such a convincing scat singer and because she had many followers, she was responsible for bringing bebop to an audience that otherwise might not have listened to it. By translating the sounds of bebop into vocal terms, she helped make a difficult form of music easier to grasp. It was the first sign of the versatility and virtuosity that she would display as a singer for years to come. ❧

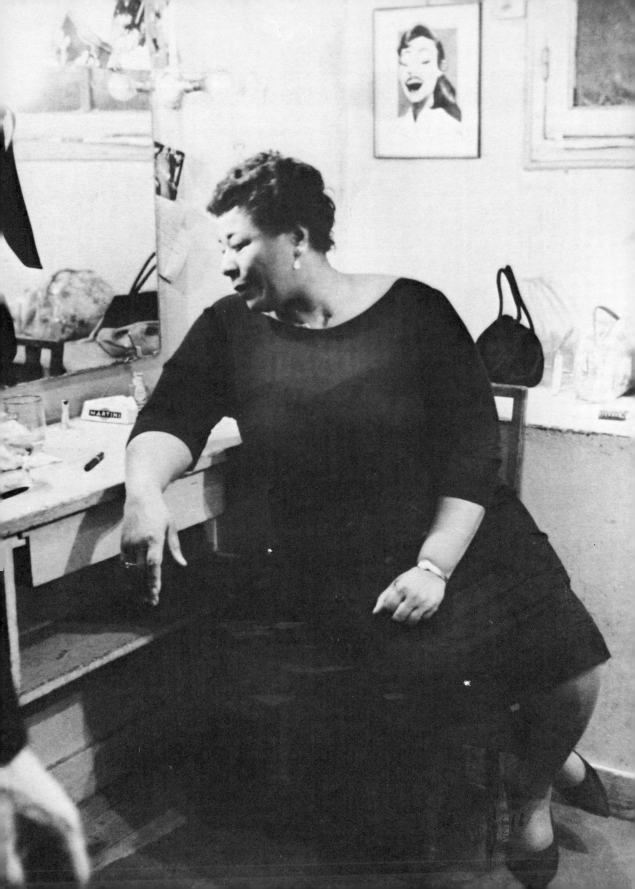

6

THE ROAD
TO THE TOP

FITZGERALD'S CAREER AND personal life both took unexpected turns in 1948, when she visited a small nightclub in Akron, Ohio. She did not go to the club because she was scheduled to perform there; instead, she went to the club to see Ray Brown, who had directed the orchestra on her recording of "How High the Moon." He was playing bass at the club with a group of musicians who were touring and performing in a program named "Jazz at the Philharmonic."

While Fitzgerald was taking her seat, she was recognized by the audience, who urged her to go onstage and sing with the group. With a smile, she agreed to their request, and her performance brought down the house. Hearing the reaction, Norman Granz, the young promoter in charge of the group's tour, asked the 30-year-old singer to join his traveling troupe, and she consented. A major reason why she agreed to join the tour was that she was about to be married to Ray Brown. Shortly after their marriage, the couple bought a home in Queens, New York, and adopted a son, Ray, Jr., who was born in 1949.

Fitzgerald's decision to work with Granz ultimately turned out to be one of the most important choices of her career, for he became a respected and influential figure on the jazz scene who helped to make her popular around the world. Barely 30 years old at the time of their first meeting, he was already well

Fitzgerald has spent much of her career traveling to different concert sites around the world. She is shown here taking a break in a backstage dressing room while on tour.

71

Fitzgerald's second husband, bassist Ray Brown, was already a member of the "Jazz at the Philharmonic" tour when she joined the troupe in 1948.

known for his commitment to jazz. He was also well regarded as someone who was willing to fight for the rights of blacks.

A native of Los Angeles, Granz began organizing informal jam sessions at California clubs in the early 1940s. The lineup of players changed nightly; musicians joined the jam sessions when they did not have to work somewhere else. Because Granz was confident that these shows would be well received, he insisted that all of the club owners follow his rules: The musicians had to be paid on time; the audience must be seated to prevent dancing and ensure listening; and the club must be racially integrated.

Granz's attempt to prohibit racial segregation was a unique action for a jazz promoter in the early 1940s. At that time, racially integrated audiences were still an uncommon sight at most jazz performances as separating blacks from whites remained the norm in most aspects of American life. Granz's request that the clubs be integrated not only enabled black and white patrons to sit alongside one another but made sure that *everyone* had the opportunity to enjoy the music equally.

Granz's promotion of jam sessions in small clubs proved to be successful, and he soon graduated to promoting jazz in large theaters. His first big show was a benefit at the Los Angeles Philharmonic in 1944, and it was a triumph. He then continued to hold concerts at the Los Angeles Philharmonic on a monthly basis, promoting shows that featured many of the musicians who had played at his first concert in the music hall. Eventually, he decided to take the musicians on the road, calling the tour "Jazz at the Philharmonic" after its original home.

Granz had a number of reasons for organizing a jazz tour across America. "I felt there was something lacking," he said. "Nobody was bringing together the great musicians." Yet he also had a second, more important motive: civil rights. In the program notes for each "Jazz at the Philharmonic" show, he placed the following statement:

> Jazz is America's own . . . deriving much of its inspiration and creation from the Negro people. Jazz holds up no superficial bars. . . . As in genuine democracy, only performance counts. . . . It is an ideal medium for bringing about a better understanding among all peoples.

Granz was determined to use the medium of music to break down ignorance and prejudice wherever he could. No matter where his musicians played, he demanded that they be treated with respect. He made sure that they traveled first-class and stayed at the

Music promoter Norman Granz organized the "Jazz at the Philharmonic" tour to foster racial equality as well as to help make jazz better known around the world.

best hotels. And just as he had done when he first promoted jazz concerts in small clubs, he insisted that his shows be open to mixed audiences, with blacks and whites seated together. He even put a clause in his contracts barring discrimination in ticket sales and segregated seating. If an objection was raised, he and his musicians could refuse to play and still be legally entitled to half their fee.

Although Granz missed out on thousands of dollars in bookings from concert hall owners who refused to book his shows or play by his rules, he got his way more often than not. "I had a strong show," he insisted, "and when people want to see your show, you can lay some conditions down." The changing roster of artists included such jazz greats as pianist Oscar

Saxophonist Lester Young (second from left) was just one of many notable musicians who played with the "Jazz at the Philharmonic" troupe. He is shown here in 1949 with fellow jazz artists (from left to right) trumpeters Max Kaminsky and "Hot Lips" Page, saxophonist Charlie Parker, and pianist Lennie Tristano.

Peterson, saxophonist Lester Young, trumpeter Roy Eldridge, and drummer Buddy Rich.

Between 1944 and 1957, the "Jazz at the Philharmonic" tour flourished, drawing enthusiastic crowds wherever it stopped. Two times each year, the troupe traveled across America on a 10-week tour, stopping at 50 or 60 cities along the way. Granz and his musicians also made excursions to Europe on a regular basis. In all of their travels, the performers never appeared before a segregated audience, and their concerts in some areas marked the first time ever that blacks and whites sat side by side in public.

When Fitzgerald joined the "Jazz at the Philharmonic" tour in 1948, she began a new stage in her career. Performing in many cities and towns for the very first time, she sang for more people than ever before. Even though much of her time was spent in transit, she never seemed to mind the grueling pressures of life on the road. A true professional, she gave herself completely to a performer's way of life and its accompanying joys and sorrows. From her first days with the tour, she had her fair share of both.

Fitzgerald's worst experiences on the tour occurred mostly in the southern towns and cities that resisted Granz's promotion of racial equality. In Charleston, South Carolina, the people in the audience were so horrified by the idea of mixed seating that they kept on staring at one another and neglected to applaud for the performers. After the show ended, the band was run out of town by a group of angry, racist whites.

In Houston, Texas, where racial segregation was strictly enforced by the authorities, Fitzgerald watched in fear as the police broke into the troupe's dressing room between sets. The police promptly arrested all of the musicians, who had been shooting dice, and arrested Fitzgerald as well, even though she had only been watching. She was taken to the police station in tears. "There were lots of things back then that

Fitzgerald listens to "Jazz at the Philharmonic" pianist Oscar Peterson during a rehearsal for the troupe's appearance at the Royal Festival Hall in London, England.

Fitzgerald was one of several members of the "Jazz at the Philharmonic" troupe to be charged with a misdemeanor during a stop on the tour in Houston, Texas. A claim was later made that the charge was racially motivated.

you either had to overlook or you got angry and cried about," she said. All of them were finally bailed out of jail by Granz, who was charged with running an illegal gambling house.

On each occasion that the members of the "Jazz at the Philharmonic" tour confronted prejudice, an attempt was made to thwart it. When a hotel manager in Ohio tried to forbid the tour's black and white musicians from sharing rooms, Granz went to the local chapter of the nation's leading black civil rights organization, the National Association for the Advancement of Colored People (NAACP), and saw to it that a story about the incident was printed on the front page of the town newspaper. The hotel promptly fired the manager.

On another occasion, Granz sued an airline company for discrimination after it bumped Fitzgerald and some other musicians off a flight. (Their first-class reservations were supposed to prevent such a circumstance from occurring.) The company insisted that the ouster was just a clerical error. Yet Granz and his troupe managed to win a large settlement from the airline out of court.

Such incidents took their toll on Fitzgerald. "Regardless of where you go," she said, "you're going to find people who are like that and you can't stop a person's thinking." But racial prejudice was not the only trouble that she encountered during her years with the "Jazz at the Philharmonic" tour. In 1953, she and Ray Brown decided to divorce after having been married for almost five years. Although they continued to be friends with one another after the divorce, Fitzgerald was hit hard by the failure of their relationship. "I guess I pick them wrong," she said.

Despite these setbacks, Fitzgerald's years on the tour also brought her much joy. While performing all across the United States and in Europe, she made friends and won new admirers wherever she sang. "I don't think I'd ever give up the tours," she said. "Being on the road gets rough sometimes, but I'd sure miss singing to the people."

Not only did the "Jazz at the Philharmonic" tours satisfy Fitzgerald's love of singing, but they also served to exercise and develop her talent. Just as singing with Dizzy Gillespie had stretched her musical abilities, so had the tours given her innumerable opportunities to improvise with other musicians. The tours,

An international success, Fitzgerald and the "Jazz at the Philharmonic" tour are warmly welcomed to Paris, France, upon their arrival for a series of concerts.

she said, were where she "really got her good education about jazz."

By the mid-1950s, Fitzgerald had been across America five times, to Europe three times, and to Japan once. She was singing better than ever, and her stature as an influential artist was soon confirmed. In 1954, she was honored for her many accomplishments at Basin Street, a New York City nightclub, by her peers. While her friends in the entertainment industry—including Eartha Kitt, Pearl Bailey, and Harry Belafonte—helped her celebrate, she was presented with a stack of congratulatory telegrams from such jazz luminaries as Louis Armstrong, Benny Goodman, and Lena Horne.

During the course of the evening, Fitzgerald was also given 16 separate awards, including tributes from *Ebony*, *Jet*, and *Billboard* magazines as well as from several foreign jazz publications. Perhaps the most significant award that she received was from Decca, her record company. Since she had started recording for them nearly 20 years before, the company had sold 22 million copies of her songs.

Even more honors were destined to come her way. In the midst of this night of achievement, Granz had a notion that would make her an even greater success.

7

"I'M GOING VERSATILE"

ELLA FITZGERALD WAS the greatest singer of their time, Norman Granz said to the 36-year-old vocalist as the "Jazz at the Philharmonic" tour took a flight to Japan in 1954. And yet, he added, she had not received the recognition that she truly deserved. With this last point in mind, he offered to become her manager, and he was willing to work without pay for an entire year just to show her how much faith he had in her.

Fitzgerald nervously accepted Granz's offer, yet she need not have worried. The following year went so well for her that she paid him even though he had said he would work for free. In fact, the working agreement that they reached in 1954 marked the beginning of a professional association that has lasted until the present. "She and I have no contract, just a handshake," Granz has said. "Mutual love and respect is all the contract we need."

When Granz became Fitzgerald's manager in 1954, he had a plan to broaden her appeal and increase the size of her audience through record sales. Until the previous decade, all records were played at 78 revolutions per minute and contained only a few minutes of music. The music industry was then changed by the development of a microgroove disk that played

According to conductor Arthur Fiedler, "When Ella performs, something very special happens: her voice becomes the orchestra's richest and most versatile sound."

81

After becoming Fitzgerald's manager in 1954, Norman Granz found a novel way to feature some of her distinctive vocal qualities on record by asking her to sing show tunes. The ultimate result of his management was that she became a more popular singer than ever before.

at a speed of 33⅓ revolutions per minute. The development of this long-playing (LP) record enabled performers to capture an entire symphony or a long jam session on a single disk.

Granz was quick to understand that long-playing records could be extremely beneficial to the growth of jazz. Before long, he was recording portions of the "Jazz at the Philharmonic" shows and releasing them on disk. These records marked the first time in music history that albums featuring the sounds of jazz cap-

tured "live" at concert performances were sold to the public.

Although Granz's first live recordings of the "Jazz at the Philharmonic" sold well, he was dismayed nevertheless. On all of the recordings, he had to cut out the parts of the shows that contained Fitzgerald's voice, for she was still under contract to Decca Records and was not legally allowed to record for anyone else. In effect, Granz could only manage half of her career: booking her concerts and arranging her tours. He did not have the right to pick out songs for her and tell her what kind of records she should make.

Although this arrangement proved to be successful for a while, Fitzgerald eventually grew tired of it. Much of the material that she recorded was not suited to her abilities. Sometimes, it never caught on with the public. "I don't know what they're doing at the record company," she maintained. "I never do get a chance at the songs that have a chance. There must be something I can make that people who buy records would like to hear."

Granz was anxious to give Fitzgerald that chance. After becoming her manager, he tried several times to sign her to Verve, his own record label, but Decca refused to release her from her contract. The situation finally changed in 1955, when Decca was preparing to release the soundtrack to *The Benny Goodman Story*, a film that featured several musicians under contract to Granz. He said that he would permit them to appear on the soundtrack only if Decca gave up its rights to Fitzgerald. The company relented, and a new phase in her singing career soon began.

Granz was determined that Fitzgerald, a classic American singer, should record classic American songs: Broadway show tunes. Because these songs were then regarded as lightweight and insubstantial works, they were rarely performed by popular singers. However, Granz believed that a good number of the tunes were

The "Jazz at the Philharmonic" tour leaves the United States for Europe in 1956. Among the bandmembers were (clockwise from bottom) Flip Phillips, Gene Krupa, Roy Eldridge, Fitzgerald, Herb Ellis, Illinois Jacquet, and Dizzy Gillespie.

The first songbook recorded by Fitzgerald featured the Broadway show tunes of composer and lyricist Cole Porter, whose songs initially became popular in the late 1920s.

written by some of the country's most talented songwriters and composed one of America's most significant contributions to the world of music. "I felt at the time the tunes ought to be done," he said, "and that the best person to do them was Ella." He believed that her recordings of the theatrical composers' works, which he called "songbooks," would spotlight her talent as well as theirs.

The first songbook that Fitzgerald recorded was devoted to the witty and stylish songs of Cole Porter. Recorded in Los Angeles in early 1956 with the Buddy Bregman Orchestra, the two-record set included "Night and Day," "I've Got You Under My Skin," and 30 other titles. Issued on Verve, the album was an immediate success, selling 100,000 copies one month after being released. *The Cole Porter Songbook* put Fitzgerald at the top of the charts and became the 11th best-selling album of the year.

But *The Cole Porter Songbook* was more than just a hit record. It was an event, marking the first time that a popular songwriter shared the billing on a record with a popular performer. Demonstrating that the singer and the composer were equally worthy of attention, Fitzgerald's album was truly a celebration of American popular music. "Where would she be if it weren't for Cole Porter?" columnist Murray Kempton said of Fitzgerald, only to point out: "But where would Cole Porter be, now, if it weren't for Ella Fitzgerald."

Cole Porter's "Begin the Beguine," featuring dancers Eleanor Powell and Fred Astaire, is staged for the finale of the film Broadway Melody of 1940. *Fitzgerald introduced a new generation of listeners to the composer's works in 1956.*

Composer Ira Gershwin (right) assisted Fitzgerald in preparing The Gershwin Songbook. *Also shown here are his collaborator, brother George (center), and dancer Fred Astaire.*

As Fitzgerald moved away from her usual jazz stylings and took a straightforward, almost classical approach to Porter's songs, she was not without her critics. She noted, "Sometimes the [jazz] fellas say, 'What's the matter, Ella, you goin' square?' and I tell them, 'I'm not going square, I'm going versatile.' " Many of her interpretations of show tunes have since become regarded as the definitive versions thanks to her willingness to display her versatility. Indeed, it has been suggested that more listeners have been introduced to Porter's music by her album than by any other recording.

Fitzgerald followed up her success with *The Cole Porter Songbook* by putting together other songbooks in subsequent years. Among the composers whose works she recorded were Harold Arlen, Jerome Kern, Johnny Mercer, and Richard Rogers and Lorenz Hart. Each songbook helped music lovers to rediscover a talented songwriter while offering audible proof of Fitzgerald's consummate vocal abilities. In 1958, she was given a Grammy Award—the top honor bestowed by the National Academy of Recording Arts and Sciences—for *The Irving Berlin Songbook*. This award was the first of many Grammys that she would receive in her career.

The concept of a songbook was most fully realized when Granz and Fitzgerald decided to tackle the songs of George and Ira Gershwin. After a full year of preparation with the help of Ira Gershwin, they chose 53 songs for Fitzgerald to record from the Gershwin brothers' more than 500 works. When *The Gershwin Songbook* was finished in 1959, it became an extravagantly packaged, five-record set. After hearing the final result, Ira Gershwin said, "I never knew how good our songs were until I heard Ella Fitzgerald sing them."

Despite having a relatively expensive price tag, *The Gershwin Songbook* sold more than 150,000 copies. Such spectacular record sales helped to expose Fitzgerald to audiences who had never heard her before. She said, "In addition to jazz singing, I had something to offer people who wanted to hear the pretty songs." Yet the trade-off worked both ways, she realized. "What's good about it, too," she said, "is that now I can also sing jazz for people who never listened before."

Fitzgerald had already captivated many jazz listeners several years earlier, when she collaborated on a songbook with Duke Ellington and His Orchestra. Boasting a sharp slant on jazz, the songbook contained 37 tracks that featured a few musicians on some

Duke Ellington (shown at the piano) said of Fitzgerald's ability to interpret a composer's work, "She captures you. . . . She's just plain good."

Shaping the course of jazz with his innovative improvisations, trumpeter Louis Armstrong was perhaps the most influential of all jazz musicians. He and Fitzgerald teamed up to record an album in the 1950s.

songs and the complete orchestra on others. The recording sessions, which began in 1956 and were finished a year later, were often hectic because Ellington insisted on perfectly played accompaniments for his longtime friend. "With Ella up front," he said, "you've got to play better than your best."

In 1957, Ellington also composed and recorded a work that he entitled "Portrait of Ella Fitzgerald." A piece that lasted for 16 minutes, it contained various movements—"Royal Ancestry," "All Heart," "Be-

yond Category," and "Total Jazz"—that were designed to evoke her through the music as well as to salute her. The two performers celebrated their work together on April 6, 1958, when they gave a joint concert at New York City in Carnegie Hall. The show was just one of many successful appearances that they made together.

During this period, Fitzgerald also made recordings with another jazz legend: Louis Armstrong. For the album *Ella and Louis*, which featured popular tunes, she demonstrated her usual generosity. According to Granz, "She insisted that [Armstrong] select the tunes, and sang them all in his keys even if they were the wrong keys for her." In addition to their album of popular songs, Fitzgerald and Armstrong also recorded a songbook of sorts in 1957: a two-record set of selections from George Gershwin's classic American opera, *Porgy and Bess.*

For Fitzgerald, the year 1957 also included a fair share of unsettling moments. During the middle of a performance at the Paramount Theater in New York City, she had to be rushed to a hospital for an emergency operation on an abdominal abscess. (She later admitted that she had felt sick during the performance

Fitzgerald with one of her many fans, actress Marilyn Monroe, at a jazz club in Hollywood, California.

After more than a dozen years of performances, the "Jazz at the Philharmonic" tour came to an end in 1957. Fitzgerald is shown here on the tour with saxophonist Illinois Jacquet.

but had not wanted to cancel the show.) While she was performing in Atlantic City, an escaped mental patient (whose last name was, coincidentally, Fitzgerald) jumped onto the stage and began to attack her.

Despite these incidents, Granz's gamble continued to pay off. After having recorded 237 songbook tracks, Fitzgerald was in demand everywhere. While continuing to appear in jazz clubs, she was booked into elegant supper clubs. She sang with symphony orchestras as well as with small jazz groups.

Fitzgerald performed in such eminent places as the Fairmont Hotel in San Francisco, California, and the Mocambo in Hollywood (thanks to actress Mar-

"I don't know of anybody in show business, black or white, who has done as much," said television personality Ed Sullivan, "to entertain audiences throughout the world as our friend Ella."

ilyn Monroe, who phoned the club's owner and suggested that he hire the singer). In New York City, she was featured at the Waldorf-Astoria Hotel and became the first black artist to headline at the Copacabana nightclub. She also made several appearances on television, which was then in its early years as a popular medium. "All those songbooks helped me to get into spots I'd never been able to play before," she said.

In 1958, Granz saluted Fitzgerald for her tremendous success by staging "Ella Fitzgerald Night" at the

Hollywood Bowl in Los Angeles. An audience of 22,000 attended the festivities, which were highlighted by her singing to the accompaniment of a 108-piece orchestra. Just as she had been during the swing era, she was again virtually everyone's favorite female vocalist.

Fitzgerald's adaptability had served her well, as it had in the days of bebop. Having made classic recordings that widened her vocal range and won her a mainstream audience, she could point to the second half of the 1950s as a period of great fulfillment. A highly visible example of black achievement, she said that those years "were like a whole new beginning for me." ❧

8

THE LEGACY OF LOVE

AMERICAN POPULAR MUSIC changed dramatically in the early 1960s, as both soul music and rock and roll began to dominate the record charts, pushing jazz and show tunes—Fitzgerald's specialties—into the background. Although the advent of soul and rock affected the extent of her recording career, her fame went undiminished. In fact, the passing of time enhanced her reputation. From the 1960s to the present, she has often been singled out as a survivor of the changing music scene.

Although Fitzgerald continued to receive acclaim in the 1960s, winning Grammy Awards in 1960 and 1962, it was a transitional time for her just as it was for the rest of America. The firmly established moral order was being challenged on many fronts, with the civil rights movement bringing tensions in race relations between black and white Americans into sharper focus and a generation of rebellious youths protesting against the conservative ways of American society. The rise of gritty soul music and hard-driving rock and roll reflected this desire for social change.

One of the transitions that involved Fitzgerald took place in 1961, when Granz sold Verve to another record company. Although he no longer owned her record label, he remained as her manager despite having stopped promoting the "Jazz at the Philharmonic" tours several years before. And she continued to perform all around the world.

Fitzgerald remained in the public eye during the 1960s by continuing to give concert performances as well as by making television appearances—including the program shown here, with entertainer Frank Sinatra.

95

Fitzgerald is presented with a Grammy Award for 1962. The award marked the seventh time that she was named top female jazz vocalist of the year.

However, the heavy touring and accompanying fatigue eventually caught up with Fitzgerald in 1965. At a concert in Munich, West Germany, she suddenly stopped singing and had to have someone lead her offstage. "We were running from one town to another," she said, "and I began to feel like I just couldn't take it." Her doctor thought that the 47-year-old singer might be on the verge of a nervous breakdown, so he advised her to cancel all of the shows that she had scheduled for the rest of the year.

"It's not easy for me to get in front of a crowd of people," Fitzgerald once admitted. "It used to bother me a lot, but now I've got it figured that God gave me this talent to use—so I just stand there and sing." Yet her dedication to achieving her goals as a singer has been so great that she still suffers from the pressures of stage fright. Norman Granz has said, "I have never seen her do a show when she wasn't nervous."

Fitzgerald retreated to her new home, which was in Beverly Hills, California, and kept herself busy with her friends and her teenage son, Ray, Jr. The amount of time that she took off as a performer proved to be beneficial. Her strength returned quickly, and she resumed making records and concert and television appearances, although at a less hectic pace than usual.

Despite these appearances, Fitzgerald's career remained dormant during much of the middle and late 1960s. Her music sounded somewhat old-fashioned when compared with the new, rocking sounds that were sweeping the country. As a result, she did not forge any new hit records, although she made a number of recordings.

Realizing that the music scene was undergoing a change, Fitzgerald did her best to appreciate the new wave of sounds. In various interviews, she expressed her enthusiasm and admiration for a number of young musicians and singers, including Elvis Presley, the Beatles, Marvin Gaye, and Stevie Wonder (whom she called "a young Duke Ellington"). Yet she did not try to imitate them. Instead, she elected to stick to pop and jazz—music that she loved and with which she felt comfortable.

This decision to keep on singing pop and jazz eventually turned out to be a shrewd one. In the 1970s, there came a general resurgence of interest in jazz—especially in jazz sung by Fitzgerald—that has lasted until the present. Recording once more on a regular basis, she became one of the first singers to be featured on Pablo Records, a new jazz label which Granz founded in 1973 and named in honor of artist Pablo Picasso.

Fitzgerald's new material included a number of Brazilian-flavored songs as well as studio sessions

The rise of rock and roll, which significantly changed the American music scene in the 1960s, was first popularized by singer Elvis Presley, who had emerged as a recording star in the previous decade.

with Count Basie and His Orchestra. Although the type of songs that she recorded continued to vary in style, her voice sounded as good as ever. Music critic John S. Wilson observed that she "might be entering an autumnal blossoming in which she reaches audiences and performance levels that were beyond her before."

By the mid-1970s, Fitzgerald began to receive a great many tributes in honor of her contributions to the world of music. She received honorary degrees from Yale, Dartmouth, Howard, and other prestigious American universities. In 1974, the University of Maryland dedicated a new facility on campus to her: the Ella Fitzgerald Center for the Performing Arts. Serving more than 1,000 students at a time, it was

Fitzgerald and Norman Granz depart from a jazz festival held in Italy, where she performed in 1971 even though she was suffering from eye trouble. A cataract was removed from her left eye later in the year, and surgery was required for her right eye the following year.

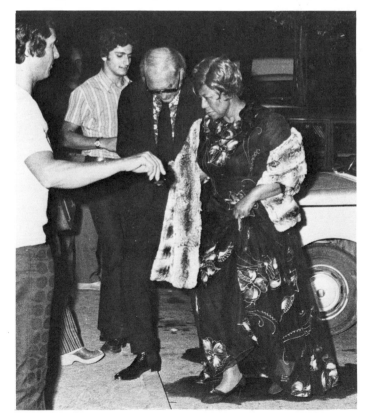

one of the first buildings in the country to be named for a black artist.

The following year, Fitzgerald shared top billing in a series of concerts with vocalist Frank Sinatra and the Count Basie Orchestra at the Uris Theater in New York City. The demand for tickets resulted in a price of $40 for the top seats, setting a Broadway record as the most expensive theater seats sold to that date. To hear Fitzgerald sing had become more than a pleasurable experience; it had become a major event.

Television gave Fitzgerald additional exposure via a commercial that she made for Memorex tapes. To demonstrate how accurately the tapes recorded sound,

Fitzgerald sings "Just a Closer Walk with Thee" at Duke Ellington's funeral in 1974. "I had known him ever since I was a girl," she said of her longtime friend.

In 1982, Fitzgerald was named Woman of the Year by Harvard University's Hasty Pudding Club, the oldest theatrical group in the country.

the commercial featured her singing, with the pure sound of her amplified voice shattering a glass. After a tape recording of her voice shattered yet another glass, the advertisement mused, "Is it Ella, or is it Memorex?"

The Memorex commercial became quite popular and made Fitzgerald a familiar figure to people who were ordinarily not jazz fans. Among those new fans were thousands of children in Columbia, South Carolina, who attended a concert given especially for them by Fitzgerald. The impressive power of her singing was not lost on the young music lovers—except, perhaps, for one boy, who said (according to the vocalist), "'Well, I liked her singing all right, but she didn't break no glass.'"

After Fitzgerald was honored at the Kennedy Center in 1979, additional awards continued to come her way in the 1980s. She received the Rose Award from Lord and Taylor department stores in 1980 for being "the person whose outstanding contribution in their field has enriched all our lives." Harvard's Hasty Pudding Club named her Woman of the Year in 1982 and presented her with a large, colorful basket (to commemorate "A-Tisket, A-Tasket"). In 1984, she received the Whitney Young Award from the National Urban League, a community service organization that helps blacks and other minority groups. Among her other accomplishments in recent years, she has helped to establish a child care center in Los Angeles that bears her name.

Fitzgerald has received a number of honors more than once. At one point in her career, she won the award for "Best Female Jazz Singer" from *Down Beat* magazine 18 years in row. She has been named "All-Time Favorite Jazz Singer" 13 times by *Playboy* magazine. And she has collected more Grammy awards than any other female jazz singer.

Although the 1980s have brought Fitzgerald many accolades, she has experienced serious setbacks as well. In July 1986, she fell ill at a hotel in Niagara Falls, New York, and was rushed to a local hospital, where she was treated for congestive heart failure. Her tests revealed that she had not suffered a heart attack, so she was released from the hospital a few days later. A spokesman for the hospital claimed that 150 callers had phoned to ask about her condition, including one call coming from the White House.

Three months later, Fitzgerald had to be readmitted into a hospital for open-heart surgery. A coronary bypass was performed on her. Although she responded well to the surgery and went home just two weeks after the operation, the gravity of what she had been through cast some doubt on the future of her singing career.

Fitzgerald remained at home for the next nine months so she could recuperate. It was, she claimed, the longest amount of time that she had stayed away from the microphone. When the doctor finally gave

Fitzgerald is awarded an honorary Doctor of Music degree by Yale University in 1986—more than 50 years after she made her first appearance there with the Chick Webb Orchestra.

"Even at this late date, one should not take Miss Fitzgerald for granted," music critic John S. Wilson said as the 1980s were about to begin. She is shown here celebrating her 63rd birthday following a concert performance in New Orleans, Louisiana.

his permission for her to attend a singing rehearsal, she was overjoyed. "It felt so good," she said. "I had spent so much time . . . wondering if I'd ever sing again."

By mid-1987, Fitzgerald was ready to perform in public once more. Among the concerts that Granz had carefully chosen for her was a show at a summer jazz festival in New York City that had special significance for the vocalist. Originally held in Newport, Rhode Island, and called the Newport Jazz Festival, it was the first major jazz festival ever presented in the United States. Over the years, the festival had expanded, moved to various sites in New York City, and undergone several changes of name and sponsorship. Yet no matter whether it was called the Kool Jazz Festival or the JVC Jazz Festival, Fitzgerald almost always performed a set. Consequently, her appearance at the 1987 festival was not only to be a comeback of sorts but a homecoming.

One week before the 1987 festival began, President Ronald Reagan presented Fitzgerald with the National Medal of Arts in recognition of her lifetime achievements. Reflecting on the award, she said, "I think of the way we used to ride the buses going to the one-nighters and everything and coming through the years and finding I not only have the fans of my day, but the young ones of today. It means it was all worth it."

The fans who came to the jazz festival on a warm June evening in 1987 seemed to agree. As the lights were dimmed and Fitzgerald moved slowly onto the stage, they rose and shouted loudly, filling the festival hall with wild applause. Waving her handkerchief, visibly moved, she told the audience, "I am so happy to be singing, you don't know." The years had chipped away some of the refinements of her voice, but its strength was undiminished. She breezed happily through two sets.

At one point in the show, in between two songs, Fitzgerald said (mostly to herself), "This is where it all started." After her nervous debut on a New York City stage more than 50 years before, she was back again, wowing the crowd by doing what she did best. "The only thing better than singing is more singing," she once observed. In 1987, this was as true for her as ever.

In the period that has followed this comeback performance, Fitzgerald has continued to reveal why she is such a unique figure in American music and why she has been so good for so long at a number of musical styles. According to music critic John Rockwell, "She brings together the major influences that have shaped American popular music in this century. Her style is not just a combination of pop and jazz, but of white and black, girl and woman, voice and instrument." Yet it is not only that she has done so much but how consistently she has done it that is impressive.

Fitzgerald receives the National Medal of Arts from President Ronald Reagan at the White House in 1987.

Throughout her life, Fitzgerald has always displayed a special affinity for children. She is shown here surrounded by young fans at the Ella Fitzgerald Child Care Center, which she helped to establish in Los Angeles, California.

Full of lighthearted feelings and warmth, Fitzgerald's voice is perfectly suited to the lively sounds of jazz. She has never sung the blues; the sad, world-weary feelings that are part of the blues seem to be foreign to her. She prefers to have her music lift one's spirits.

Some of this lift comes from Fitzgerald's masterful technique, but much of it comes from the personality of the singer herself. The feelings that she translates into music and passes on to her listeners are a result of the kind of person she is: sincere, positive, and uncomplicated. She has never sought refuge in drugs, liquor, or fast living. "She has remained one of the few singers for whom the typical American goals remain normal," critic Leonard Feather observed.

Along with her singing, Fitzgerald's devotion to her goals (amidst one of the busiest careers in show business history) is an achievement that continues to be widely appreciated throughout the world. "Just don't give up trying to do what you really want to do," she has said. "Where there's love and inspiration, I don't think you can go wrong." ☙

APPENDIX

SELECTED DISCOGRAPHY

Ella Fitzgerald's incredible versatility as a singer is revealed in the following albums. For anyone who is not familiar with her voice, these highly recommended recordings should serve as a good introduction to her music.

Princess of the Savoy (1936–1939) (MCA Records)

Ella Sings the Band (1936–1939) (MCA Records)

The Best of Ella (MCA Records)

The Best of Ella Fitzgerald: Volume II (MCA Records)

Ella Fitzgerald Sings the Cole Porter Songbook (Verve Records)

Ella Fitzgerald Sings the Irving Berlin Songbook (Verve Records)

Ella Fitzgerald Sings the George and Ira Gershwin Songbook (Verve Records)

The Duke Ellington Songbook (Verve Records)

The Duke Ellington Songbook: Volume II (Verve Records)

Ella and Duke on the Cote D'Azur (Verve Records)

Ella and Louis (Verve Records)

Porgy and Bess (Verve Records)

A Perfect Match—Basie and Ella (Pablo Records)

Ella Abraca Jobim (Pablo Records)

CHRONOLOGY

April 25, 1918	Born Ella Fitzgerald in Newport News, Virginia
1934	Wins amateur night contest in Harlem
1935	Makes first professional singing appearance; joins the Chick Webb Orchestra and is legally adopted by Webb
1938	Cowrites and records "A-Tisket, A-Tasket," her first hit record
1939	Webb dies; Fitzgerald assumes leadership of the band
1940	Fitzgerald joins the American Society of Composers, Authors, and Publishers (ASCAP)
1942	Appears in her first film, *Ride 'Em Cowboy*
1947	Tours with Dizzy Gillespie
1948	Marries Ray Brown; meets Norman Granz and joins the "Jazz at the Philharmonic" tour
1949	Adopts Ray Brown, Jr.
1953	Divorces Ray Brown
1954	Granz becomes Fitzgerald's manager
1956	Fitzgerald records her first album of show tunes, *The Cole Porter Songbook*
1958	Receives first Grammy Award
1979	Honored at the Kennedy Center in Washington, D.C.
1986	Undergoes coronary bypass surgery
1987	Awarded the National Medal of Arts

FURTHER READING

Colin, Sid. *Ella: The Life and Times of Ella Fitzgerald.* London: Elm Tree Books, 1986.

Dahl, Linda. *Stormy Weather: The Music and Lives of a Century of Jazzwomen.* New York: Pantheon, 1984.

Dance, Stanley. *The World of Swing.* New York: Scribners', 1974.

Feather, Leonard. *From Satchmo to Miles.* New York: Stein & Day, 1971.

Fox, Ted. *Showtime at the Apollo.* New York: Holt, Rinehart & Winston, 1983.

Giddins, Gary. *Riding on a Blue Note: Jazz and American Pop.* New York: Oxford University Press, 1981.

Gourse, Leslie. *Louis' Children: American Jazz Singers.* New York: Morrow, 1984.

Haskins, James. *Black Music in America: A History Through Its People.* New York: Crowell, 1987.

Pleasants, Henry . *The Great American Popular Singers.* New York: Simon & Schuster, 1974.

Schiffman, Jack. *Harlem Heyday.* New York: Prometheus Books, 1984.

Simon, George T. *The Big Bands.* 4th ed. New York: Schirmer Books, 1981.

Ulanov, Barry. *A History of Jazz in America.* New York: Viking Press, 1954.

INDEX

110

PICTURE CREDITS

BUD KLIMENT lives in New York City and works for the Pulitzer Prize Board at Columbia University. He specializes in film and music writing and has contributed to the *Village Voice*, *Video*, and other periodicals. His writing has also appeared in *The Book of Rock Lists*, *The New Music Record and Tape Guide*, and *The Virgin Guide to New York*.

NATHAN IRVIN HUGGINS is W.E.B. Du Bois Professor of History and Director of the W.E.B. Du Bois Institute for Afro-American Research at Harvard University. He previously taught at Columbia University. Professor Huggins is the author of numerous books, including *Black Odyssey: The Afro-American Ordeal in Slavery*, *The Harlem Renaissance*, and *Slave and Citizen: The Life of Frederick Douglass*.

DATE DUE

MAY 3			
ILL 10-2-98			
FEB 24 AM			
JAN 3	2012		
GAYLORD			PRINTED IN U.S.A.